# WORD SALAD

# Word Salad

Poems tossed by

## PHIL POCHUREK

LUMINARE PRESS
WWW.LUMINAREPRESS.COM

Word Salad
Copyright © 2024 by Phil Pochurek



Printed in the United States of America

Luminare Press
442 Charnelton St.
Eugene, OR 97401
www.luminarepress.com

LCCN: 2024919635
ISBN: 979-8-88679-689-6

# With Thanks

I would like give thanks to Lee Enry. It was her sharp pencil and even sharper eye that help bring Word Salad to a readable version of my poetry and letters. She has painstakingly gone over every word twice to make sure no matter how strange or absurd my thoughts may be at least they are technically correct in their delivery. Helping me share my thoughts, feelings and experiences clearly and correctly. She is my most devoted fan. Lee has cleaned up my pages grammatically when my words would get tangled up in the page and when they tried to escape out of the margins and off the pages themselves. When I handed Lee Word Salad it looked like the picture on the back jacket and when she was done it looked like the front cover. As for what goes on between the covers, you will have to judge for yourself. Three score of time in my travels have brought me to this season in my life. I'm blessed to have arrived here now in one piece... so far. With eyes wide open I am ready to accept the consequences of my choices wherever they may take me. This book is a collection of my notes along the way as I have seen, felt and experienced them. I am thankful for Lee's gentle guidance and dedication in helping me bring them to you.

"Poetry is the paint on the brush
That colors our lives.
The aroma of life
That adds flavor to our days
And seasons our nights.
The light that helps us to see
The pulse of the world—
When it seizes the mind.
Opens the heart and
Frees the soul...."

# CONTENTS

## PART TWO

# The Dressing



## PART THREE

# The Best of the Rest

## The Life We Choose

## The Other Side of the River



## Everyone Has a Story

# Preface

## Word Salad: Poetry?

Word Salad poetry is a random collection of word thoughts lived, observations and events (past, present and future, made) not necessarily in that order, thrown together at someone, meant to get their attention or create a distraction. Meant to stimulate conversation in the abstract. In a spontaneous fashion or moment. A piece of word bling thrown at you by someone teetering on the edge of narcissism with an aphasia escape clause. A mumble of word thoughts without the alibi of a head injury or stroke. Occasionally striking gold in a phrase. Thoughts, feelings and observations thrown together with pen and paper as a painter of watercolors would do. Adding colors and using water to see where it goes. Word Salad takes the reader on a word-trip to convey a vision to the eye of the beholder or in this case from the poet, on paper, to the reader. A bare spot in my wiring occasionally wears through, electrifying and unfiltered. Hitting a nerve. Touching a feeling. Shaking a memory loose, long forgotten or still fresh and tender, maybe even on the mend. Word Salad has no beginning, middle or end. Each poem belongs unapologetically to itself. Tide pools of words gathered between these pages are from an ocean of memories, seventy years in the making, and the tide is definitely on its way out. Broken pieces of dreams, some realized and others missed are saved, salvaged and gathered between these pages for your entertainment. Take them on, sort them out, and see if anything makes sense to you when you're done. "Word Salad anyone?"

# PART ONE

# Word Salad

# Aminotique

In an instant I'm off on a journey
Back to a place where it all began.
A place where all thoughts
Become breath and motion
As I jump into a soothing pool
Of warm water with a splash.
The wholeness of everything
I've grown to become
Washes over me and engulfs me...
Touching every pore, every memory
Every experience I've ever had
And can remember—
Sometimes things I've long forgotten.
Probably from another time, another life.
Every day starts now in the comfort
Of these early morning hours.
In the pre-dawn light
Before the rest of the world
Has begun their day, in the water
I get a little head start
So I can keep up when
The rest of the world starts to move.
The dark silence is comforting.
The warm water soothing,
Reminiscent now to every muscle, every nerve
And every thought as I began to wake them up.
Easing them into the rise of the sun
And the pulse of the world,

With every breath, every stroke I take.
In the water my spirit runs free.
Off leash and collar
From my flesh and bones that restrain it,
As I go through out my day.
Water is the connection
To my soul in the morning and my waking hours.
In the night, it's my dreams.
In the water I swim, float, and flow through
Rivers of thoughts and feelings
On their way to an ocean of
Memories and experiences,
People and places...
Past, present and what may lie ahead.

In my dreams I fly!
Soaring high above the present
Through time and space.
Consumed by landscapes
Familiar and new.
Over and through them
Fantastique and surreal.
To new frontiers and old events.
Behind scars that sometimes
Remind me of things
I can't seem to forget!
Often waking up heavy



*Phil Pochurek*

With the sweat of remorse soaking the sheets.
Too late to be forgiven—
Stubborn lessons never learned.

But the water is more forgiving,
More gentile, as it holds you
While your spirit floats around you.
Only holding on to you
By the rhythm of your breath.
An invisible umbilical cord
That reminds you,
You're in the world of now and
You're on the clock.
Your spirit times out
By how long you can hold your breath
To let it flow free.
A wash in the memories
Of how it was before there was you,
Before you had a name
To live up to, to live on for
In this time, in this world.
In this flesh and blood...
That is strangely unique.
At 5 a.m. the water calls my spirit
Home to what it knows best.
Home to the quiet peace
Of the water, it's Amniotique.

# Bits and Pieces of a Dream

Teeth and tits,
Knees and hips...
Once they're in your body, they're yours.
No one needs to know.
No apologies required and no regrets!
Parts that wear out
Can be replaced
Where function and beauty are desired.
We may be God's perfect machine
To that I have no doubt
It's perfect in every way.
But when things break down—
Rip, tear, or fall out
It's up to us to say:
Put them back in, make it right, take it out,
Make it new one more time
To help us move, help us eat,
To let us see
And get up off our seat!
The way we use to do,
The way we use to be,
When things were new.
When we could move,
When we could chew.
Like we did before the fall
Of a broken hip.
Before cancer took a nip

Out of a breast.
Before the drugs reached beneath
Your dignity, your gums, to take your teeth,
Or maybe you just want to smile again
And feel the relief without any shame,
And share your joy with the world
And the time you have left.
With the people you meet.
The people you love.
To be the person you use to be.
To be the one you've become,
The new one everyone can see.
From the way that your clothes fit
To the spring in your step.
The smile you give
From your eyes,
When you flash your teeth
To the people you meet.
All just maintenance on God's own machine.
For all those who want to keep on going
For another day, a week, for years.
Fixing the parts in dis-repair that held you back

                    *Phil Pochurek*

From being the person you once were
To being the new one you've become.
The one you've earned, the one you deserve,
By living for so long.
It was time to make things right!
Tighten a screw, fix a break,
Make something new again, it's all right.
No one needs to know.
It's all part of you now
That gets you through your day,
On your way to being
The one you were meant to be.
In a new old fashioned way.
It's okay to fix all the bits and pieces
Of God's perfect machine
When they wear out.
That's when you begin
To finish living your dreams,
Keep moving, keep seeing, keep smiling...
And savor what life is all about.

# Cat Soccer

Cat soccer?
That's what I thought!
Who thinks this stuff up?
Well apparently, my cat "Bob" does.
Certainly not me.
I got introduced to it
Just standing there
Making my morning cup of coffee.
When all of a sudden
My cat politely tapped my foot,
Which is how the game starts.
Because his little whiffle golf ball
With the little bell inside
Has been put right on top of my foot!
No matter how I moved
It was game on!
My first mistake.
So half-awake I flick it away
In Messi fashion.
Before I can pour my coffee, he's back
In a flash! Eyes on fire
And full of passion!
This is going to be fun.
I used to play soccer too!
Though some adjustments will have to be made,
Some memory reflex was still there.
Then I learned "Cats Rules".
The more I tried

To advance the ball,
The faster he retrieved it.
By now I've put down my coffee
To prevent unnecessary spills
Trying to score...
LMFAO around the kitchen
And onto the dining room floor.
With tears in my eyes
I was amazed at his
Lightning speed and reflexes.
Clearly, I was out matched!
That's when I realized
Cats don't have a sense of humor
They have sharp claws,
Whose evidence of sharpening
Is all around the house;
Apparently in preparation
For games like these.
It turns out cats are very competitive.
They play to win and to eat!
It was coming to me
That by the blood on my socks
(all mine) not Bob's,
I'm not sure which one
Bob was considering—
Eating or winning!
Winning at Cat soccer

 *Phil Pochurek*

Is the indoor version of killing
For food and sport outdoors for cats.
His skills are inherent.
The proof is in the blood in my socks!
Proof he has no respect
For red or yellow cards, either.
So, for my sake we switched
To the squirt bottle!
Something he could understand.
We played all around the house.
Only occasionally stopping
To retrieve the ball from
Under the couch or behind the bookshelf.
Don't ask it happens, no corner kicks.
His stamina and focus are unmatched,
Which brings more tears
From laughter and pain!
With more blood, more squirting required,
Which eventually brings a stop
To the game for first aid.
Bob gets a nap,
And I get Band-Aids
And more coffee.
It was a painfully great game
About catitude and competition,
Until we play again.
Bob won....

# Eulogy

We spin, we float,
We fly through life
Until one day we drop where we are-
Whatever we were doing,
Wherever we were going.
To go where we've been headed all along.
All on a timeline unknown to us.
In a plot so thick
Only God knows how it will all end.
In the pattern of a snowflake,
In the passing of a cloud.
From the sound of the wind
Through the trees.
Do we ever realize when the mighty ocean
Has calmed its roar,
So we can hear the hissing of the water
In the sands by the sea?
Flattened its crashing waves
Upon the shore
To see if anyone has noticed?
When we stand on the stump
Of a fresh cut mighty tree
You can feel the ghost of
Of where it used to be,
Where a long life had once stood.
Count the rings and we can see
Where a life long-lived had been.
Feel a time that was,

That lived, that came and saw everything
Before you and me.
As we gather in this moment
To remember this life that was
Close to us, a blood part of some of us,
Let us gather now
One in love as they depart.
Count their rings
As we remember them.
The ones wrapped around our hearts.
On this day we hold them close,
As we gather round together as one now,
To count their rings and know
They're with us always.
In our hearts and minds
Everywhere we go.
Every time we remember them
They're alive again...
Who they were
And where they've been.
Let the memories they leave behind

          *Phil Pochurek*

Be the ones that make you smile.
Live on in the moments
That give you joy and hope.
Last a long while till
One day we meet again.
Have peace of mind in knowing
When our time comes
To leave the world behind,
When the Lord comes to call us home,
That they'll come for us.
To be with us, to take us
Where we're going...
And we will be with them
In the house of the Lord,
Forever.

# The Last Crossing

In the pre-dawn hours
The streetlights lit the road
Same as they do at dusk,
As the sun slowly brings the day.
Only this morning would be different
For someone's family, in a terrible way.
About halfway down the road
Before the turn I take
Heading towards the city pool
For my morning swim,
There was something in the road.
A horribly beautiful sight.
The lifeless form of a cat
Lay breathless and still.
Where only the day before
I had admired its grace and beauty
When I slowed to let it pass.
As I drove by, I realized
What I must do, out of respect.
I turned my car around
Put on my hazards and
Blocked this lane from view
In one direction.
I couldn't let this beautiful life
Be desecrated by repeated crushings
From more indiscriminate drivers
Without so much as a care.
Once was bad enough.

It broke my heart to take the time
To physically touch what would soon become
The meaning of someone else's despair.
Her fur was soft, well-kept and loved.
No sign of trauma could be seen.
And with the absence of blood
It was hard to tell
If this cat wasn't asleep.
But death had come in an instant.
A flash of light with a glancing blow.
I quietly began to weep.
No sign of breath or purr
That comes with the warmth
Of love and life.
She was cool to my touch
And death's stiffness,
Had just begun to settle in
As I gently lifted her
And placed her off to the side of the road,
Which looked like the side of the road

     *Phil Pochurek*

She had come from so many times before.
Maybe she was just trying
To return home,
To the home she has no more.
My heart went out
To those still asleep
At home inside their beds.
As the sun began to rise.
Whose hearts unknown to me
Are waiting to discover death's token.
To find their beloved kitty
Asleep beside the road in death,
Whose hearts will soon be broken.

# Help Me Please! I Can't Remember Everything Before I Can't Remember Anything

Somethings changed, shifted,
Different than the days before-
In the last weeks, months, few years?
Things I use to remember with ease
I can't remember anymore...
Now slip away or go blank more often
Then I can recall, then dissolve into tears.
Bits and pieces of events and places
Explode like shattered glass
Into shards of memories,
And some of them I can't remember at all.
I used to keep my pencil pretty sharp
In case there was something
I needed to know or should recall.
Now I'm lucky to remember where my pencils
Even are or anything at all.
Thank God for Siri and Alexa!
And for our habits, patterns and routines
That get us through our days.
That help keep us in our grooves...
Let us stay home a little longer
Before someone says we have to move-
One more time.
From all the things we have and know
And all the things we've done

That have gotten us this far
All come down to: being on our own;
Taking care of ourselves in the end;
Living alone; when we should
Stop driving our car;
Buying groceries; taking our meds;
Doing our laundry and making our beds—
Are all the things of everyday life.
Of course, it's easier
If you're lucky enough
To have a husband or a wife,
Children or grand children,
If you're so blessed
Before they tend to slip away
And float down their river of life-
As they should.
Occasionally checking in to see
If you're still here and okay.
It's nice to get a phone call
Once in while or a drop in visit
Just to let you know
You're not forgotten,
And that someone still cares.



*Phil Pochurek*

Hopefully maybe a heads-up
Call first so they don't
Catch you sitting around in your underwear
Drinking a beer.
It's funny how they get to decide
If it's safe for us to be on our own.
When did they become the parents
And we become the children
Left at home, alone.
When did they get to start making up the rules
To keep us safe and in line.
From being a member of
The rising class of
"Seniors Gone Wild" all the time.
But everyone may not be lucky enough
To have been married or have kids
That check up on them in their day to day.
Or maybe they had someone
Who shared their life with them
But has gone on ahead and passed away.
And left them to finish on their own.
"Help me please!"

I've forgotten a few of the little things
To get me through my day to day.
So what if sometimes I can't remember
Where I put something when I put it down
Or I forget to put it away-
It doesn't mean I can't be left alone!
I've come too far down life's long road
To end up in a damn nursing home...
I'll find me a minder, a gentle reminderer
To help me find what I need when I need it
Then put it back where it belongs when I'm done
Before they go home.
A part-time watcher
And sometimes finder, that's all.
Someone who might just happen to be here
In case I should happen to fall.
A fatal signpost to getting old.
Long after the keys and the burners are gone.
Someone to show me the way
When I can't find my way home.
Instead of calling an ambulance
To come and take me away.

        *Phil Pochurek*

# I Can't Remember and I Don't Know

"I can't remember," asked "I don't know."
"What time is it?"
"You mean today?"
 Said "I don't know."
"Yes!" said "I can't remember!"
"Then I don't know!"
"What time is my appointment?"
"Which one?" said "I don't know!"
"I can't remember!"
"Well then, I don't know!"
"You're supposed to keep track of my appointments!"
"It's either my doctor appointment
 Or my dentist appointment!
 Which one is it?"
"Which one did we go to last?"
"I can't remember."
"Then I don't know."
"Don't you ever write anything down?"
"Yes of course I do."
"Well, where's your list?"
"I can't remember."
"Well, I'll ask Siri! She'll know!"
"Who's Siri?"
"I can't remember"
"Then I don't know."
"Let's have some ice cream!"
"All right then, I like ice cream."
"Where should we go?"

"Go where?"
"I can't remember."
"It's okay. If you can't remember
 Then we won't go."
"Go where?"
"I don't know...."
'Lets have ice cream."

  *Phil Pochurek*

# In the Locker Room

In the locker room
There is no mercy.
Everyone sees things just as they are.
Sagging skin, bulging muscles,
Hair or not where it shouldn't be
Where it use to be.
Every wrinkle, every scar
Has a story.
Young and old are
All different, all the same—
Versions of God's perfect machine.
In the locker room
All pretenses are dropped
When your towel hits the floor,
And there's nothing between you
In the light of your naked truth.
Everyone's looking
And nobody cares, but you.
We're all God's children
In God's view.
The locker room is just a test.
We're all the same in different ways.
No one's better or worse
Than the rest.
Only God knows the whole truth.
All we can do is be our best.

# Just Us

There comes a time
When the kids are full grown,
Long moved out and on their own.
Lost in the jet stream of their full-on life.
Some get married, have kids
And buy a home.
While others keep searching
And continue to roam,
Making a life of the search
Toward their unknown.
Dreams they hope to find.
Some settle down, take root and find their groove.
While others fly free and continue to move
In search of what their looking for–
Whenever they figure out what that is.
As long as they're safe and happy
Who could ask for anything more?
That's all that matters to me.
Who they are and what they become,
And who they turn out to be
Has long been up to them.
I may not always have what they need,
But they'll always have my love.
I can give them all the money I have,
But until they earn it
That's when they'll see,
That the best things in life are still free.
I like to think

When we were still young,
And they were so small
I feel we got the best years of their lives...
From diapers to walkers then movers and talkers
We could catch them when they'd fall.
It's a long journey down the path they're on
From that beginning to their end.
Sorting out their wants
From their needs along the way,
I hope I taught them well.
We taught them what we knew.
Planting in them our seeds of love
Because that's what parents do.
How they've grown and choose to love
And care for those around them
Reminds me why I love you.
As all the seasons come and go
And the years pile on like drifts of snow,
We begin to feel the weight of time
On our bones, in our minds, and it begins to show.
In our step, in our hair, and our eyes.
The days on the calendar begin to fly by,
And that's when we realize and begin to know—
People we knew who shared our past
Begin to disappear and die...

          *Phil Pochurek*

And time seems to go so fast.
Where did everyone go?
Everyone's in such a hurry now,
We can see it as we begin to slow down.
To take in the moments as they come.
In photos we can remember some
As our memories begin to fade and become undone.
But what do you do
When there's no one left to ask,
Because the only one left, is you?
Our daily routines and habits
Give us purpose now,
And determine where we go,
What we do and for how long.
Sometimes if we even can, anymore-
I'm so glad that I'm blessed to still have you.
Each day begins as the one before,
At least we can only hope it does.
Breathing, moving, starting our day
Without any pain as if there never was
A reason to think otherwise,
And everything still works okay.
When the morning comes and the coffee's made,
And I look into your eyes,
I'm still lost in the love of you.

That's all that matters to me now.
You're the only person I trust anymore
In the world's daily fuss
At the end of the day when all is said and done,
And the world winds down for the night.
I thank the Lord as we count all our blessings.
We made it together for one more day-
When all that is left is just us.



*Phil Pochurek*

# My Laptop Has Fur

I'll never not have or go without
The weight of warm fur,
Purring in one continuous
Breath on my lap.
The silent joy it brings me
Almost defies description.
Pure love conveyed in a vibration
Without words, in contact
Through touch, sound and heat.
The love, empathy, and joy it radiates
Is visceral, tender and sweet.
Visions, flavors, and aromas are
All rolled into the weight of fur
As they're poured into my ears
And run down into
The seat of my soul.
Bringing peace to the moment.
Calming my thoughts and stilling my mind.
Until I can no longer read, concentrate or focus.
I go blank behind closed eyes,
A drift in a sea of content.
Afloat in a moment only to be broken
By the sudden jolt
Of a launch to capture
An annoying fly in midair!

For a morning snack.
Abruptly bringing me back
To the world of life and death,
Love and joy,
And my cat.



Phil Pochurek

# Questions

How many years lie ahead?
Will they be remembered or forgotten?
Will we have time to atone for them
Before we're dead?
When will you forgive me for the things that I've done,
For the terrible things that I've said?
When will the time come that you will forgive me,
Bury the hatchet and put them to bed?
How long will these grievances last?
How can our love ever move forward,
When you can't let go of the past?
How many more years do I have to tell you
I'm sorry for all the things that I've done,
That hurt you and caused you so much pain?
When will you believe me when I try and tell you
I don't ever want to do any of those things again?
I've run out of reasons for saying I'm sorry
For all those things I did so long ago.
I've tried to be better in all things about you,
But I'm running out of time and this much I know...
I can't change the past and all that I've done
That have hurt you along the way.
If we can't move forward and let go of the sorrow
Then I've run out of things to say.
It doesn't seem to matter what I do—
The thread has been broken that held us together,
But that doesn't mean that I don't still love you.
There are too many years between us for that.

You've become all that's left of my heart.
I hope that someday you can forgive me
For all the reasons that drove us apart.

# The Apology

In the presence of your joy,
In a moment of desire,
I lost my grip.
I could no longer hold back
The wild child in me,
And I kissed your tender lips...
Where so many words
Have been spoken
To hearts that were healed by them
Where they had been broken.
I tasted the sweetness
Of your soul that lingered there
After every word,
Like a choice red pomegranate
Ripe for the picking.
I went lost in your eyes
And dizzy in the sweet
Fragrance of you.
I became the impetuous boy-child
Who couldn't keep himself
From doing something
He knew he shouldn't do.
When I stole a kiss from your lips
I tasted the light in your soul,
From the deepest part of you.
Where the words that are warmed by your breath
Are carefully chosen and spoken with love,
As an artist chooses every stroke of his brush.

Painting a picture of what's in his heart.
When you spoke I broke in two...
Hoping for forgiveness
For acting without permission,
That you might forgive my trespass.
Rather than suffering your denial
Upon my request, I took a risk.
And the wild little boy in me
Couldn't keep from helping
Himself to you any longer.
In a moment without words,
In an act of sudden passion,
I lost myself in the presence of you
And stole a kiss...
Betraying my true intentions.
That boy has since been sent to his room!
Awaiting permission to receive your decision
On what his punishment should be
Before his release!
As we beg your pardon for his
Uncontrolled act gone amiss.
With regret I must admit
We are one in the same,
As we ask for your forgiveness.
We humbly apologize, and accept
Whatever punishment you decide.
And willingly take the blame.
We broke your trust,
When we crossed the line
To steal a kiss for the both of us
For two hearts that are one in the same.

     *Phil Pochurek*

# The Bob Zombie Cat Zoomies

Back and forth,
Up and down.
Over and under
And all around!
It's no use.
He's a relentless little shit,
And I'm captive to his abuse!
There's a near death
Experience about to happen.
I can see the rainbow bridge in his eyes!
So, it must be time to get up.
The zombie cat zoomies are on.
One minute he's here,
One minute he's there.
One minute he's here,
One minute he's there.
But reach for him
And he's gone. Surprise!
He's like a two-year old
Toddler with claws.
I can't explain it!
There's no reason for it.
Some nights are just
Better than others.
If you're lucky,
You might get away
With hiding under the covers.
I think it's time

To get the dog,
Someone to keep him
In his place.
I've been too long without one, anyway.
A pup to chew him up a little.
Chase him around,
Then hold him down
And lick his face.
Someone closer to the ground
He can understand.
Maybe even kick his ass!
Someone who can take a scratchin'
And keep come backin',
Until he's finally out of gas.
The front room floor
Looks like isle nine
At the Dollar Tree store.
There's cat toys everywhere and
Always under my feet!
When I ask him,
"Who's going pick all these up?"
He just looks at me and says,
"Who cares?"

                    *Phil Pochurek*

"When are we going to eat?"
Each cat is only a kitten
For a short time in your life,
And everything that goes with it.
I thought it would go relatively fast.
Nobody ever told me
How long that might be
And the zombie zoomies would last?
The nights are the worst, sometimes...
What could possibly go wrong?
There's a squirt bottle in every room.
Especially one right by my bed!
Just in case the cat zombie
Comes calling on Bob
In the middle of the night
And starts messing
With my head.

# The Last Garage Sale of Ella Wanda And Janet Grace

One sold everything she ever owned.
Sentimentality was something
She never bemoaned that could be
Easily sold or replaced.
The other saved everything
She ever owned and saved your stuff too,
If you left it alone.
She had stuff stashed all over the place.
They laughed and partied off and on
Like any mother and daughter would,
But most of the time
They fought and screamed
And believe me it wasn't good.
Sounded like pigs being slaughtered.
You could hear them
Fighting all the way down the street.
Mostly simple things you know:
That's yours? That's mine?
Have you had anything to eat?
Did you take your meds this time?
Maybe we could sell some of this stuff too?
"No not that." "It doesn't belong to you." "It's mine."
On went the rows.
As they sold things and made change,
Constantly bringing things
Out to the table.
Mom loved to sell things

To make a little money
When she was able.
But my sister never did,
And she didn't think it was funny!
It was harder for her to let things go,
So she saved it all...
And bought more,
And the reason she did
The Lord only knows.
Now I'm the only one left
In the family to decide what goes
And what stays, and finally
To settle this mother and daughterly score.
Two women who meant the world to me
Were finally quiet and could scream no more.
Who both hated their Christian first names.
They never used them,
Felt abused if you teased them,
And scolded you until you were ashamed!
All water under the maternal bridge.
Now I'm the one who must decide
What to do with all their stuff!
Years of gathering, storing and collecting...
"Too much was never enough!"

   *Phil Pochurek*

Of course, there had to be a sale!
I'm sure my mother is laughing right now,
While my sister is screaming as she wails.
Now I'm the only one to tag, sort and sell
Everything they ever owned.
All the rest goes away to the ne'er-do-well
Except for my dad's shotgun!
It's the last sale for Ella Wanda,
But a travesty for Janet Grace—
That all her years of gathering and storing
Were for not, for nothing, and a waste!
Hoarded and stacked, she piled and packed,
Two and three of everything I'm sure—
From ceiling to floor...
Barely enough room to open the door
From her hoarding.
Death was the only cure.
And now they're both gone.
No hands to hang on to the things
They thought mattered so much.
Left it all behind for me to come find,
And decide what's worth keeping and such.
Sold to pickers what I could.
But that turned out to be no good.

They stole some things
And took more than they should.
So, I gave the rest away
To those in need.
It was never about the money.
I hope mom thought that that was funny!
I tried to do the best I could.
It's not much fun
When you're the last one
To decide what goes where,
And what stays from the last things
Of the only family you've ever known.
One more garage sale to place
All their vanities of this world
For Ella Wanda and Janet Grace.
Both gone to the wind without a trace.
As Solomon well knew
You can't take it with you,
And when you go someone else
Just takes your place.
So, enjoy what you have while you have it.
Then let it go when it's time to move on,
Because you know you can't take it with you
And it all becomes someone else's
When you're gone....

        *Phil Pochurek*

# The Weight of Water

There's a peace in the silence
  Of the weight of water.
That's when I feel like
I'm free of the world.
In the absence of gravity,
I feel the weight of the world, the past
Lifted from off my shoulders.
The water holds me to the now
Of the present moment with a single breath.
There is no past to return to,
No future to go towards.
Only the time and air
That is in your lungs in the moment,
Lifting me up to the light
Of the everywhere and everything of
All that could be all at once.
Pulling me back to an amniotic time,
Before the weight of my everyday life begins to
Weigh me down with that first step.
The first time my foot landed
Back on the ground,
And everything that goes with it...
With sweet memories of all that is right.
Giving me hope for a day
When you can discover that your joy
Has been with you
All along right where you left it.
Sometimes it just takes the right person

To shine a light on it for you,
And when you're holding them
You're at home in their arms and
Lost in their eyes...
Right where you want to be.
Cradled in the moment
Of whatever comes next.
Swimming in their security
Of everything will be all right.
And that works for me.



Phil Pochurek

# *They Them Their!*

When this and that
Met *they* and *them*
Nobody knew who was what,
Or what was when
And how many there really were!
Until *they* showed up
To set things straight that
*They* came with him and her.
*They* finally cleared the air
As strangers often do.
It didn't matter now
Because this and that
Where outnumbered by *them*—
The count was four to two.
I'm not sure how
This whole thing started
Or when it all began
That our kids became so confused?
Between what *they* was
Or what *their* wanted to be.
A woman or a man.
So, *they* became whatever
The moment called for.
Why just settle
For one thing or the other
When *they* could be so much more?
Who would of thought?
When *they* were young

And we told *them* you
Can be anything you want to be—
*They* would take us at our word!
So, they broke the mold
And said you're on,
And headed off into the absurd!
When one thing led to another
And "their" became a new thing!
Living life in the plural
Would shake things up
And never be the same.
Keep everybody guessing
What you are today?
If you're one or two,
And make sex just one big game.
Life in the plural is so much more
Than just being who you are.
Why be one?
When you can be so many
And become an Internet star!
How soon we forget
That long ago it was all done before!
When nothing you can say
Will turn this tide,
Paint a red stripe over your door.

          *Phil Pochurek*

The fall of Eden
Was only the beginning.
Now it looks like the end has begun.
Someone let the lion in this circus
Out of his cage and set him free!
And now look at what he's done.
No one knows
What's up or down.
Who is what?
If your head is in the sky
Or your feet are on the ground.
*They* will tell you to forget everything
That came before you were born,
Because that's what *they* like to do.
If you were born in the thousands
And bring any history up
Chances are *they* won't believe you, anyway.
Between the Internet and AI
How can you know if it's true?
All that matters now is
What happened five minutes ago to *them*,
Because that's what they like to do.
Or what will happen
Five minutes from now, because
All the rest may not be true.

"Let the old people believe in
All of that old stuff!"
*They* live in the past anyway,
Because that's what old people do.
It's the only thing *they* know.
That's all *they* ever talk about with you
Whenever *they* get together,
Everywhere *they* go."
And that's why it's hard
To say the words
To turn this ship around.
When everyone's afraid
Someone might shout or melt.
Don't rock the boat,
Just go along or else
You may fall out... of likes!
So next time you decide
To go out from behind
Your all powerful, magical screen
Where real people actually are—
Be careful what you say to who!
Things aren't the way they used to be,
The way they were yesterday
For me and you.
If you don't already know

              *Phil Pochurek*

The answer to your question
Before you ask it,
Then things are better off left unsaid.
Because they'll never be the same again.
Where once upon a time
You could look at someone
And tell if they were a woman or a man,
And everyone took the same chances.
Now *they* and *their* get to decide
Who is what and where is when?
It's all too confusing for me.
I'm sorry for those who date today,
Looking for old fashion romances
The way things used to be.
It's a whole new dating game.
But I'll take my chances
The old-fashioned way just the same.
I was born in the thousands,
So I don't mind dating
The way things used to be.
I'm not so good at the pronoun game,
But if it works for you
That's okay with me....
Please don't get mad if I get it wrong
Who's *they* or *their* supposed to be.
I'll just ask them, then wait and see!

# Weather or Not

Welcome to Miami
With all this humid rain.
Only this is Oregon
Without the hurricanes.
Warm and wet this summer,
Cold and moldy in the fall.
What everyone thinks is a bummer
Could mean no forest fires at all?
Yeah, right!
It's hard to light your sparklers
In the middle of the pouring rain.
I'm older now, so it doesn't matter
If I ever light another sparkler again.
I use to worship the summer
And all that sun on my skin,
But now it's time to pay the price
And hope that cancer doesn't set in.
It's hard to tell the difference
From the late spring summer rains
Which season this really seems.
But the leaves on the trees are the dead give away—
From the golds and reds of autumn
To the vibrant, verdant greens of spring.
Windows open to the sound of the rain
And all the peace it brings—
Far outweighs the heat of the summer sun
And what it does to me now, and my skin.
So, you won't hear me whine or complain.

Whatever the weather the seasons bring
All are good days...just the same.
And I'm happy with what I've got.
One more day to take a breath...
Rain or shine, weather or not.



*Phil Pochurek*

# The Last Romance

Everyone's forever is different.
No one's heart is the same.
We cast our lots with the best of intentions
From what we know,
From where we came.
From all the days we've lived and breathed,
And all the seasons come and gone.
For all the things that we got right
To all the ones that we got wrong,
There was always love in the end.
Everyone's forever is different.
We think what we want is what we need,
And we have to have it if we want to succeed,
But nothing could be further from the truth.
As we look back with wise old eyes,
How easily we can see
Through our disguise
To the folly of our youth.
So, we chase the butterflies of our dreams.
Occasionally catching them only to find
They weren't always what they seemed,
And our joy bled out into the truth.
That all things end we thought would last.
Even those we've loved and held so dear
In time they too would come to pass.
Everything we see that is alive
Is a miracle to behold,
And will one day be dust in the wind.

We're lucky and blessed if we can survive
By the grace of God to get old in the end,
And to have learned from our mistakes.
To share our blessings
With those we love
By giving them all away.
I saw the end this afternoon
When I kissed death today-
And everything became crystal clear.
I still had time to make a difference
And forever only lasts
While you're still here.
Everyone's forever is different.
It's time to let go
Of all things that can end.
Things that can break, go missing and rust.
Then open your eyes, your heart and mind...
To give to the Lord all your trust,
In the precious time that you have left.

     *Phil Pochurek*

The boldest truth in life is death,
But love lives on in memories told
From all the treasures of our years.
To remind us all as we grow old
Through all the laughter and the tears
That time is in the air we breathe.
Our clock starts when we take our first breath,
Then stops when it's our time to leave.
When all that's left of flesh and bone
Will soon return to dust,
To live on in your stories retold.
Where love and truth
Are all that last
Of how we lived and what we believed.
Cast in memories made of gold
Until our forever comes to pass.

# When Grand Dames Meet

When two grand dames meet
It's like two great rivers merging.
Think of the Amazon and the Nile
That could converge just before the sea.
To share their travels, their journeys,
Their moments across time,
And their histories together.
It is a privilege to behold.
When all that's left now hidden
Behind the wrinkles, the cracks and creases,
Etched into their faces
Behind fierce blue eyes
Are two dried and mighty riverbeds-
To tell the story of their traveled lives.
Where vibrant and raging waters
Once rushed and flowed through a time
That they both lived through,
But many didn't survive.
When the world was a different place.
Bent and slowed now in their present days
The memories of their mighty waters, their waves
Still run strong through their beating hearts.
In their stories and words
They tell from bygone days.
From the tragedies and remnants
Of world wars and a depression,
They persevered through life
With glamour, power and grace.

Careful not to lose faith
With a sparkle in their eyes
When they speak,
And a smile on their face.
Shinning bright from their hearts
Where embers still burn-
That can be traced from memories lived
In their stories told from long ago.
Times and places, they both passed through
With all their troubles, joys and cares,
From a time now only, they can know.
Things must have seemed
Like magic when they happened,
At the times when they both were there.
To see them, sometimes survive them
At the same time everywhere.
In a much closer proximity
Unbeknownst to each other at the time
Then they could have ever imagined.
Had they only known...
All things they both saw and knew.
Each a memory now
Rises up from the cracks

          *Phil Pochurek*

In their mighty riverbeds.
Exposed to each other
In this moment, on this day.
Lost in the shared memories
Of each other's waters.
Of a time now and a place
Only they can know.
Because they were there.
Each memory pieced together in this shared moment
Of their collective past.
With smiles and laughter, they wrestle to recall
Their places in time, together, over tea.
Two mighty rivers sip and chat about
The waters they once lived in and knew.
Whose currents are etched on
And written in their hearts,
Behind the faded blue of wise old eyes
That can see straight through to your heart,
But sometimes go missing in their minds
As they remember them back to you.
There's a sweet reflection of the beauty
And the strength they both once knew
Chiseled deep in their porcelain skin,

That goes lost in the wrinkles
Written on their faces
That even time can't erase.
When two grand dames meet
In the joy of their surprise,
There's still fire in their hearts
And a sparkle in their eyes...
From shared memories of a time and place.



*Phil Pochurek*

# Where Did Wednesday Go?

It used to be the number
Of the day that I would lose,
But then the day itself
Would go missing on its own!
Sometimes when I "waked" up
Not sure what time it really was?
Alexa would always know "hands free,"
Just because.
But when Wednesday goes missing, blank, gone—
Then the days seem out of order
And I would always get lost.
It made the week a little shorter
Or longer, depending on
Which end you looked at first.
One way might make you feel better
But the other way a little worse.
Lately it seems to be Wednesday that goes missing
As far as weekdays go,
I'm beginning to think it's a curse.
I know what the beginning and the end look like,
It's the middle where I get confused.
And lately I just can't seem to get it right!
When Wednesday goes missing, gone, out of sight—
I feel like I'm being calendrically abused!
It's a strange feeling
Standing in the middle of the week
In your underwear
And not know what day it is

Without a care.
Seems like yesterday
It was only Tuesday,
I remember it pretty well.
And it feels like tomorrow
Is going to be Thursday,
But only time will tell.
So, what happened to Wednesday?
I'll be darned if I know!
I think I got up and did something,
But right now I can't seem to remember.
I just can't know.
I've tried to remember
And looked all around
At where I'm at but
Any signs of it are gone.
So where did Wednesday go?
It's a funny day sitting
Right in the middle of the week.
When you look back
You can see the beginning
And forward to the end,
But when I look around



*Phil Pochurek*

At where I'm at
I just go blank again.
Wednesday seems to be the one day
That I forget the most,
Every time I wake up there
I feel like I'm a ghost.
I get lost trying to find my way
Until Thursday shows up
To start another day,
And Wednesday is gone for another week.
Then it all starts over again.
When Monday and Tuesday roll around,
And Wednesday plays hide and seek.
Why this calendar conundrum picks on me
I guess I'll never know.
When I go to bed on Tuesday night
Everything seems to be okay though...
Until I wake up the next morning
On Thursday and wonder
"Where did Wednesday go?"

# Word Salad

Slowly as we ripen through the years
And into our old age,
We begin to break down and wear out
From across all the seasons of our lives.
Through all the sweetness and lows,
The laughter and the tears
Rise up from the bottom
Of our collective hearts.
Then our livers begin give out and
To litter our gossamer skin
With banana peel freckles.
Blue spider like veins pulse
Through translucent skin
Across the landscape of our bodies
Like roadmaps to show
How far we've come-
And where we've been.
Our skin breaks easily, rips, and tears often.
Bruises from the slightest bump
Are slow to mend and long to heal.
We bruise easily and deep
All the way through to tired bones
Too brittle to feel.
Deep and dark like a Georgia peach
Sat too long on one side in one place
And now too late to eat.
And that's just what we can see.
From a gentle bump

On the way through a door,
Or a scrape that we didn't even notice before
Until it starts to bleed.
So, we begin to wonder
When's it all going to end?
Where does this all lead?
While inside our broken minds
Our thoughts head off
Around the bend without us...
Sentences begin to fill up with blank spaces.
Words and places, people and faces
We've known the whole of our lives
Become redacted.
Slip out of line and go dancing
In the margins, to the borders of our memories
At the edge of our dreams and go
Lost in between the lines.
Just out of reach, fading off into the moment.
It's not until they come around again
Like a random spin on the wheel of misfortune
That the hopelessness sets in,
And it shows on our faces.
Until something or someone reminds us
Of where that train was going
With our thoughts.
When it slips off the track again
To something else we were thinking

     *Phil Pochurek*

Or another place we've been,
And we give the salad another toss.
We count the days now
One at a time, that's all that really matters.
Each one a blessing to its own.
Our weeks and months, years and seasons
Now all rest in the past,
Without rhyme or reasons
And we don't worry about what's to come.
Time is much too precious for that,
Our jobs long over and done.
So, we leave those days to the young.
If it looks like sun,
We may grab a light sweater
If its raining, grab our raincoat and hat
To keep us from catching a cold.
Simple things we learned along the way up
When we were young!
That's how we got to be so old.
Our animals know how long
We have left way before us you know
How it's all going to end.
They stay close to our sides or in our laps
When the end of our time begins.
They've been through it many times, before-

And when it's our time, our turn,
They can smell it on our skin...
See it in our eyes, and hear it in our voice
And remember
That's what they came here for.
To stay close to us, as we come
To the end of our time,
As we have done for them
Across the many seasons of our lives.
Babies and grandbabies, cats and dogs,
And sometimes husbands and wives—
All pass through our doors on their journey back
To where we all began.
Let my blessings be the dressing
I pour in the bowl
Over the word salad of my life.
No worries my friends,
We'll just laugh when it all begins
At everything I say.
Just point me towards the door
When it's my time to go,
And that will be okay.
I'll grab my coat and hat, and
With my dog waiting patiently at my side...
Oh! Almost forgot the cat!
We'll be merrily on my way.

      *Phil Pochurek*

# Word Salad #2

Sometimes when I sit
I try to remember something, anything, everything.
Just one thing.
Anything that comes to mind.
Something I've lost.
Something I've forgotten.
Somewhere I've been.
Something I've done.
Something I've said.
Someone I know.
Someone who's dead.
The time.
The day.
My name.
Who I am.
Where I'm going?
Where I've been.
What really matters anymore.
Am I at the beginning or at the end?
Sometimes when I sit
It's hard to stay awake...
And I wonder does it really matter anymore?
And for what?
Is this all there is?
There must be a mistake!
Or is there something more?
What was it I was looking for?

And then she smiles
Out from behind her sweet blue eyes and says
"Let's go home," and I remember
Everything all at once!
As she wheels me back inside....
Sometimes when I sit
All I think of is her.



*Phil Pochurek*

# Zodiac Bingo

Sounds like Zodiac Bingo to me.
Virgo, Gemini, Taurus, Leo... Libra. Bingo!
Two of them got away with my heart and
Three of them became my wives.
Forty-one years of marriage in total,
And I loved them all
To the end and always.
Now take me to the pool so I can linger
In the space in between
Yesterday and tomorrow...
Just for one hour—
Uninterrupted by the gravity
Of everyday life.
Weightless and free
Of body and mind.
Four dogs, three cats
And three wives
Have brought me this far
To the journey to becoming myself.
To wonder...
Is this where it ends?
Looking at what's left of my life
Through a whole different lens.
Maybe I've been living my life
On the spectrum all along
And nobody told me, I wonder.
I hope I'm wrong.

Maybe the only peace
I can find now
Is underwater... between breaths.
Of a life interrupted.
Each stroke a little death.
I wonder.
Under the surface, beneath the pain
That never really goes away,
Are the scars that can't be seen.
They just go deep
And all their questions with them.
Underneath all the please and thank yous
That get us through our everydays.
It's the little secrets
That we keep in the dark.
In the deep.
Between breaths when I swim
Are the little deaths
I try to wash away.
My Zodiac Bingo life
Is now like the holes
On a rotary phone dial... obsolete!
"I'm running out of numbers to call,"



*Phil Pochurek*

He said with a smile
As he put in the last dime he had.
"No worries, no worries at all," he said.
There's nobody home
To answer the phone anyway.
They're either not home or dead!
But he still calls... how sad.

# A Farewell to Sex

When you can't remember
The last time you had sex
Or it doesn't matter anymore,
That's sorry and sad
And both aren't good,
Because the sex isn't the same
As you remember it before.
But if you do have sex
And when you're done,
If all you are is just tired and sore
More than you had fun
Then something's not right.
When there's no joy anymore,
And sex even as an exercise
Can sometimes cause pain
Across crepe skin and varicose vein
Sometimes brittle bone,
Then sex may be safer as a bittersweet memory
And better off left alone.
Across years of passion
That burned smoldering hot
Sometimes sex is better off left
To memories untold,
Then trying to recover those embers
And make it something it's not.
Too many feelings
Can get hurt on the way
If you just can't get that fire to start.

Sometimes a memory
Is better off left to its own
When it's stored away
In the bottom of your heart.
There's a reason that sex
Is left to the young,
A subjective term for sure
As it's spread across the years.
Something so passionate, delicious and sweet
Shouldn't end in disappointment and tears.
Hidden in the closet of
The quiet and discreate.
Whether you share it with someone
Or have it alone,
It should happen with love and tenderness
And not with shame.
A moment shared between two lovers
Or a man and his wife
Should happen without asking
When it's over "if you came."
Everyone's bodies are different now.
Our hearts and our minds
Tend to go their own ways,



*Phil Pochurek*

And our bodies may forget...
As we all come into our age
The way things were back then.
It's not as easy as we remember how it was,
To get them all on the same page again.
As the sun sets on our passions,
And the crimson reds of our youth
Turn to gold as they begin to fade.
There's comfort and grace
As we grow old in the peace that we've made,
That sex we shared when we were young
Has finally found its place.
In a smile, a kiss, a gentle touch,
In the wrinkles on your face
And the words we love to hear:
"I love you darling and always have,
With or without any sex."
In a gentile whisper in your ear.

# Coffee and Kisses

She comes for coffee and kisses.
What am I going to say?
"No? I've already had my coffee." Right!
I try not to think that early in the day.
It's too easy to be stupid
And it's too early for kisses? Not!
Everything is yes.
She brings the coffee with her
Made and flavored just right,
To get the juice's flowing—
Erase the wrinkles from the night
So you can smile.
She wraps her arms around you
When you meet her at the door
And says "I had them make it the way you like it."
Then you know, "this could take a while."
Her day started long before
You ever thought of opening your eyes.
She was getting ready to taste your lips.
Soaking, washing, scenting
Every inch of her body for you.
From the tips of her perfect toes
To the smile behind her sweet, soft lips.
You never stood a chance.
You were disarmed at the door.
With coffee in hand, she's on you
In all her caramel latte sweet delight.
She comes in close to kiss your ear

And says, "it's all for you... sleep good last night?"
And you wonder if you're dreaming,
As she gently takes your breath away
Into her lips, with a kiss.
With coffee steaming in each hand
You lift and kiss her through the door
Her feet full off the ground.
For the longest moment
You hold her close and drink her in
Before you softly put her down and say
"Good morning."
All night long you wrestled with your sleep
In search of a dream
To get you through the night,
Only to wake up and find one
Standing in your door...
With coffee and kisses ready
To jump start your day.
Get all your juices flowing
From the night before.
With her sweet kisses
And coffee in hands,
I put her down and close the door....



*Phil Pochurek*

# Every Day

Every day you are in my thoughts
I see what you see,
I hear what you hear,
And I want what you want.
As the world of me
Slowly disappears into you.
I go with you into your day—
Two steps back.
In my mind, and in my heart,
And out of your way.
To protect you from harm.
All my thoughts of you
Give me joy, and comfort me
When you're not here.
I see the heart of you
In your wake, in every step you take,
Everywhere you go...
And swim in the sea of your love.
The warm waters of your spirit
Have washed over me, and healed me
From all past injuries to my soul.
After you, I have forgiven the world.

# For You

I want you to cum.
I want you to cum a lot!
I want you to cum often!
I want you to cum without guilt!
I want you to cum by yourself!
I want you to cum for yourself!
Long and deep, and feel it
From the bottom of your heart.
I want you to cum for all the years
You never came at all.
To feel your soul in all its glory.
In every inch and corner of your being.
I want you to whisper your joy.
I want you to scream, to shout your pleasure
Until you're out of breath.
Out of guilt.
Out of shame for all the times
Someone made you feel that way.
And for all the times
You never came.
I want you to cum.
For all the joy you deserve.
For all the time you've lost.
That's waiting for you
To set it free.
For all that you have suffered.
For all that you have sacrificed.
For all you have lost.

This time is for you.
I want you to cum...
With me.



*Phil Pochurek*

# Forever

Why can't I stop thinking about you?
I can't get anything done!
I can't remember simple things
I'm supposed to do.
Like put on my pants or tie my shoes—
And how much fun life is
Whenever I'm with you.
It calms me when you're in my thoughts
As I go about my day.
It gives me pleasure to know
You're in my life.
In so many wonderful ways.
All of a sudden
I want to breathe again.
Everything looks different now
Since you've come into my life.
Opened my heart to let you in.
There's an innocence
And wisdom about you
That gathers in your eyes
When you smile...
That's so inviting on your lips
That makes them have
To be kissed, a lot and often!
Something I always want to do
Whenever I'm near you
And you're within reach.
You're irresistible to me

With all your charms.
I always want to be with you.
To hold you in my arms.
Every day. One day at a time.
Forever.



*Phil Pochurek*

# I Love You Anyway

I'll never forget
The day we met
And all your everything
Was on display.
Your words said one thing
But your eyes betrayed you.
It was something
I would come to regret!
But I loved you anyway.
We all have something
We carry with us
Across the whole of our lives
That makes us who we are.
Some secrets we carry
Far longer than we should.
Holding us back to a past
To something we can't change,
And that is never very good.
Keeping you from going as far
In life as you should,
To what you could possibly be.
Stuck in a yesterday
That's always the same—
Keeping you from being free.
All your wounds have made you
The person you are today
With all their memories.
You have to let them heal though,

If you want them to go away.
Not everyone has to know
What made your scars.
I love you anyway.
All that matters now
Is that you're here with me.
Whatever it was
That broke your spirit
Has let your true light shine through
Out into the day...
That's all I care about-
And that you'll always know
I love you anyway.
Whatever it was
That hurt you then
Can't hurt you now
Or ever again.
You're not the person
You were back then,
That was all in yesterday.
So, let it all go...
And remember always
I love you anyway.



*Phil Pochurek*

# In the Flames of Desire

I long for the days
When our bonfires burned.
When your skin and bone strained
Against my flesh and I yearned
For your touch, your kiss,
Your breath panting
Against my neck–
I reveled in the fragrance
Of your heat.
The sweet salt of your sex
On my lips, on my skin,
In the sheets.
Those days we were on fire.
All those flames glow softly now,
In memories shadows hidden deep
In the secrets of our souls.
Only for us to know
That once we had it all...
Have it now as we had it then.
In a look, in a touch, in a word,
And the smile in your eyes
That says "yes" to it all
After all these years.
I love you for it now,
As I loved you for it then
And I always will
Until long after the end.

# Lost and Found

I've finally realized
I have a problem.
And that is
That I am the problem!
I'm not thirsty,
So I don't drink.
I'm not hungry,
So I don't eat.
I'm not lonely,
So I'm okay with being alone.
But...
I want to drink.
I want to eat.
I want to be with someone.
Have someone.
Share my life and live
With someone.
All that I have.
All that I am.
But...
I seem to have lost that person.
I don't know where they went,
And I don't know
Who they are any more.
Where to even look for them.
I'm tired and careless.
Missing something, someone.
I've lost my joy.

A key element in my life
That gives it meaning,
Purpose, and a reason to survive.
I've also been cut off
Cold turkey from my wellspring
Of unconditional love.
A loving lease that expired
When my last dog passed away,
And my beloved cat of 22 years
Followed not far behind-
It made me a
A ghost in my own life.
Absent without a cause.
How easy it is to
Take the air we breathe
For granted until it's gone,
And we're overboard drowning
In the sea of our own life.
Under water with only the air in our lungs
To save us, and time is running out.

That's where I found a peace in the silence
Of the weight of water
And the absence of gravity it holds.
When I go from my vertical life

                        *Phil Pochurek*

Grounded by my habits, patterns and routines
Into the weightless horizontal life of the swimming pool,
My mind is set free.
Where any thoughts and dreams
Can be examined without restraint,
To ebb and flow with my every breath.
Until I climb out of the pool
And take those first few steps
Does the weight of my vertical life
And the gravity of the world
Rest on my shoulders.
Pulling me back down into
The reality of my body and
Everything that goes with it.
It holds me down to the now
Of the present moment,
But lifts me up in the light
Of everything, everywhere all at once.
Out of the water, out of my past,
That holds me back at its worst.
Fills me up with the present at its best,
And sweet memories of all that is right.
Giving me hope for the days ahead.
While in the water I've discovered that my joy
Has been with me all along,

Right where I left it.
Sometimes it just takes the right moment
With the right person
To shine a light on it for you.
When they're holding you
And you feel at home in their arms
That's when you know
It's right where you want to be.
Lost in their eyes.
Cradled in the moment
Of whatever comes next
And knowing everything will be okay.
That's when I know I'll be all right, again.
Lost and found for one more day.



Phil Pochurek

# Only You

I love every inch of you.
Of your skin. All of you.
It radiates sweet delight.
Sixty-one years in the making.
The way it clings to your bones.
Holds everything so beautifully together
And right in place.
So lusciously smooth and tight.
It needs to be kissed all over
Continuously and often.
The scent of you is intoxicating, blinding and delicious.
It makes me dizzy
When you're in my arms.
I'm completely lost in the heart of you.
Without a word I melt
Into the smile in your eyes,
Then drown in your laughter
As I fall to the ground
To kiss your sexy feet.
I must have been lost
The whole of my life
Before there was you.
I'm so glad the Lord has
Brought me home to your arms
Before it was too late.
The only thing that matters now is time
And how much I have left in my life
To spend with you, darling.

Doing whatever it takes to make you happy.
Feel loved and safe in all that we do
For all the rest of my days and nights...
To spend them all with you.

 

# With*

***W**ith
The hardening of some attitudes
And the softening of your pride,
With
Your memories
Come the platitudes
From way down deep inside
That ring out loud and true.
Do unto all others
As you would have them
All do unto you.
With
The passing of time
We may learn to see a little more
Even as our eyes begin to fade.
With
Our lips pursed shut
We may hear something new
That we haven't heard before
That someone said.
With
All the changes going on
To our bodies and our minds
We still have time to pray,
Because we know that
There is someone listening
Who cares about what we have to say.
With...

Our heads bowed low
And our hands held high
This much we can always know.
We can count on the Lord to lift us up,
Fill our hearts with love and joy
Anywhere we go,
And be there when we die.



Phil Pochurek

# The Best of the Rest

# The Life We Choose

# The Life We Choose

There are choices in life we make
That move us along
As we go on our way.
At the time they may look like the right ones.
It's not until later when we look back
To see what we have done do we notice
That it wasn't them after all.
And we were the ones
Who got it all wrong
Even though we had won.
It isn't until later do we realize
That winning isn't always worth
The price we have to pay
For what it cost us not to lose.
All part of the lessons we learn
In the life we choose.

# The Tackle Box

The tackle box came
Down and down and down.
I can't even remember whose
Father's it was first, I only knew
It was mine now because
I was the only one left.
Fiberglass, plastic and aluminum.
It screamed the sixties, it screamed of him.
Antique plugs, hooks and lead.
I remember it like it was yesterday.
My dad carrying it down the bank
Saying everything would be okay,
And now it was mine.
There's no one left but me,
I'm the end of the line.
I cherish it who would have thought
That this would be my dad's legacy.
Every time I touch it I think of him
And all the times we had
Few that they may have been,
Some of them were pretty good,
But most of them were bad.
Every year in April,
When my license is brand new,
The tackle box is the first place I go.
I love you anyway dad...
And when I'm fishing, I open the tackle box
And think of you.

# Who's Gonna Clean My Glasses?

Everything seems fuzzy
Since that day.
Nothing is really clear.
So much has changed
Since you went away.
The only thing that
Really mattered was you–
And now you're not here, forever.
Oh, there's plenty
Of pictures and memories
To remind me of how things were.
What a grand pair we use to be.
I guess I thought this
Day would never come.
Now it feels like something's broken,
And I don't know how to fix it,
And the only one left to do it is me.
Every morning we'd have our coffee,
Share the paper and
Maybe the puzzle too...
That's when you always
Brought my glasses to me,
Recently found and freshly cleaned
All the better for me to see you.
I'm sorry now I never told you more–
How much that really meant to me.
You cared enough to
Clean my glasses every day.

It was the sweetest thing,
Just so I could see.
Now I'm lucky if I can even find them!
They're never where they were before
Or where they're supposed to be.
Now it doesn't matter if they're
Dirty or they're clean.
When I put them on and look around me
My life is empty without you, if
You know what I mean.
There's no one here to listen to
To set me straight when I get off track.
When I wander off
The beaten path and get lost,
Because you're not here
To bring me back.
I should have listened
When you told me
Some day this day would come.
I never thought I'd be without you;
I never thought I'd be the one left.
And now I sit and drink my coffee

          *Phil Pochurek*

And wonder where my glasses are?
It's funny how everything
Seems so clear.
I miss the timbre in your voice
When you made me laugh.
I miss the scent of you in the air.
Now who's gonna clean my glasses?
I really miss you now
That you're not here...
And I can't find you anywhere!
There's no one left here
That loves me like you do.
Did you take my glasses with you?
I guess when I find them
I'll clean them myself,
And when I put them on
I'll be seeing you.

# A Ghost of You

I never paid much attention
To time, before I met you.
Then the value
Of every hour, every minute
That I could spend with you
Became clear to me...
I'm reminded of
How much I miss you
When you're not here.
There's a ghost of you
In your perfume,
In the bath, from your wake,
When you left the room
Only moments before.
That is so sweet, so fresh
I can still see your image...
In the steam on the mirror
On the bathroom door
Over your lipstick kiss
That was left for me there.
And as I press my lips to the glass
For one last taste of you,
I'm reminded again
Of all the reasons
For all the things that you do...
Why I'm kissing your lips
When you're not even here.
That's how much I love you.

# The Softening

The length of years
That hardens bone, seasons wood, softens stone
Eventually leaves us less than we were.
It comes on slowly and loosens our skin,
Changes our hair, our teeth,
And everything underneath and within,
And inside our lives
As we begin to turn in.
Events and issues we use to handle
With certainty and ease.
Now we may not be so sure
Or secure in our decisions
And what we believe.
The urgency to get to
Then get through life
Seems less important than its value.
We trade possessions and money
For time and memories
Before it's too late to do
Anything but remember.
You no longer need glasses to see
What's important in life,
In others, and in yourself.
Sometimes we look back
With shame and regret at something
We've said or done and wonder
Who that person was.
It's so much easier to

Forgive someone else
Then it is ourselves
For our discretions.
In the softening we learn
To hear the music
That's been inside us all along.
To dance and let go
Of who's right or wrong
And just be who we really are.
Maybe even begin to sing
Blessed be the softening.

 Phil Pochurek

# Digital Bitches

I love my digital bitches
In a love hate sort of way.
I mean if my technology's going to talk to me
She better be nice and have something to say.
I catch my workouts when I can
On my treadmill in the den,
Where I can watch the game and get a workout
Like any other man.
That's where I met Rhonda.
She was my fitness babe in a can.
I thought her voice was okay at first
Until I didn't fit into her plan!
She told me "I'd get a better workout
If I didn't hold onto the bar".
"That's how I check my heart rate," I said,
But she didn't seem to care.
So, I politely said "Fuck you Rhonda,"
Then quietly lit a cigar.
Which brings me to my next little micro chippy.
I call her Dorthy Garmin by name,
She takes me out and brings me back
Exactly the way I came.
I thought her voice was pleasant too.
At last I could relax in my car,
Until I missed a turn and Dorthy piped up
"Recalculating" like Fran Dresher on Cozaar.
"Sorry Dorthy, I strayed a bit
And didn't take your advice".

So, the next time she said "Recalculating,"
I said, "Thank you Dorthy I don't give a shit, but that's nice".
And last but not least my cellular phone
Introduced me to a girl I call Jeannie.
My hands-free babe "Just say a command."
I like that in a girl, if you know what I mean!
So I bought an earbud and proceeded to drive,
And asked Jeannie to make a call.
"Say a command," she whispered in my ear.
That's when I clearly said "Call".
Jeannie was nice and politely replied:
"Call who?" as phone girls do.
I said "Call Bill." She said, "Call Phil." I said, "No Bill" and quit.
That's when I realized Dorthy was deaf
Or I had a lisp or cleft,
Then dialed the way I use too.
I still call Jeannie every once in a while
Just to hear her say, "Say a command."
Then hang up and dial the old-fashioned way
And finish up by hand.
Those are my girls, my electronic bitches,
That help get me through my day.
They may have some glitches,
But they keep me in stitches
In there femininely digital way.

     *Phil Pochurek*

# In The Silence of Men

As men get older they speak very little,
Unless you ask them too just right.
The less that is spoken
The more that is known goes silent.
Hidden safely out of sight, protected
And grounded from within.
Only spoken on a need-to-know basis.
So be careful when you're looking for answers,
You could get lost in the silence of men.
Asking for directions is a metaphor for retreat,
And a retreat from confidence
Is an admission of failure, a cry for help, or defeat.
Don't ask, don't tell, never will.
When in doubt don't cry out, don't cry out.
But men reach out in many ways
To help and protect, to give and support.
With little said, no thanks required—
A smile, or a hug will do.
When men love they give respect, they give hope.
They're consistent and sincere with you.
Warm in their touch and kind in their eyes.
Their meaning is clear and their tone is true.
From behind the mask of Adam
The soul of our fathers
Shines through, again and again.
All that was never spoken,
Never heard, is there and
Lives on in the silence of men.

Nobody heard the horns blaring
Of them sounding their retreat
Over the din of women rising,
Laying claim, taking over the streets.
The more that women had to say
The less that men could refute.
Their words just seem to get in the way,
Every reply was a dispute.
With victory came freedom,
But at what price have we paid?
From the boardroom to the bedroom,
To the dinner table and in the car.
When silence became the olive branch
And an unspoken treaty that was made.
Didn't anybody notice? Doesn't anybody care?
All that knowledge, all that wisdom
In all those fathers everywhere,
Lays waiting, behind patient eyes
To be realized, to be asked again.
Waiting there in the peace, in the quiet.
Hidden in the silence of men.



*Phil Pochurek*

# The Picasso Years

The finesse of time
Slows us down physically
So that patience replaces competition
As we enter a new genre of living
In our farewell to our youth.
It's a long journey to arrive at wisdom
Through experience, with our bodies and spirits intact.
Mentally, physically, or both—
Let's say whole, though most of us never do.
Depends on how hard we hold onto
The things we chose to value...
Like pride, prestige, reputation,
All fancy words for selfish instead of selfless.
Unchecked, they can poison you.
Life is a short game but we like to drive for show,
Often forgetting when you learn something
You have to be patient when you putt for the know.
We all start out with the same ingredients,
Add our own unique flavor and style to it all
To the person we become,
And hope when we reach the finish line
Our soufflé life doesn't fall.
Sometimes the clues are hidden,
But mostly they're conspicuous out in plain sight:
A shirt tail left out, sleeping till ten,
Glasses lost on top of your head.
Forget why you went in that room again?
You may know that there's something's wrong

Just not how to make it right.
Only one shower a day, maybe?
Topped off with a nursing home shave,
Just close enough to keep the crumbs
From sticking to your face
With a few random hairs left behind
That you missed because they grew misplaced.
It's the things that don't show
That are hard to find.
They're the hidden out of sight ones
Deep in the back of your mind.
Your phone number forgotten
And the car keys misplaced again.
Names and faces of people and places
Sometimes even the day of the week all erased.
When will it ever end?
It's merciless sometimes
When your own mind plays hide and seek.
But for most of us
There's someone around
To help us remember, to help us be found—
When we get lost in our conversation,
Or at the mall, as we wonder and wander
Down the long road home...
If we'll ever get home at all.

     *Phil Pochurek*

In snapshots we're reminded of the things we've done
And the places we've been, that we're not alone.
From the children we've raised to
Our friends and next of kin
Who have been with us all along the way.
In memories we all come home in pictures.
They take us back to help show us the way
Maybe help us remember
How we got to where we are today.
Often our thoughts become abstract, broken,
Filled with doubts and fears,
When our points of view become random or misspoken
Often taken out of context, can bring you to tears.
So, we start each day over
Carefully planning everything we do.
Trying not to get lost or stuck in the past—
Trapped in another lifetime, a ruse, or the untrue,
And the shadows that they cast.
Embracing the old familiar,
Instead of the present, the future, and the new.
The fading colors of the day
Bring us to the sounds and smells of everyday life.
To remind us how important every sunrise is,
Of how much sand is left in the hourglass,
How much water is left in the well.

How important each sunset is as we watch it pass.
In our Picasso years you can't always tell.
It all goes to fast as things begin to blur
Into one thought, one memory, one day,
And we're reminded again that nothing lasts
As we fold our hands to pray.
We try to color our goodbyes with grace,
With each stroke of the brush
As we put our lives in place.
Someday you'll understand.
It's hard to tell who of us
Will make it home in one piece
Or get lost along the way.
Rejoice with us and save your tears.
It's a risk we all have to take or
We'll drown in our own fears.
It's sink or swim when you enter in
The Picasso Years.



*Phil Pochurek*

# Desert Moon

It's one o'clock in the morning
In the light of an August full moon,
And it's 90 degrees, even with a slight breeze
And you're wide awake; it might as well be noon.
It's too hot to sleep
And your sheets are all wet,
So you're naked out on the deck
Using the stars for your blanket
With watermelon dripping of your chin
And sweat running down
The back of your neck.
What a delicious summer morning
For such a succulent moonlight treat.
You never looked more natural, or sexier
Than when you're naked while you eat.
I'm beginning to like this heat.
The sweat glistening on your body
Under the white of a desert full moon
Sparkles like diamonds on your skin.
While I'm tracing the outline of your shadow
With my eyes, I can smell you.
Just a hint, just a whisper of jasmine.

The desert was never more beautiful
Than it was on that hot August night,
Watching you eat your watermelon
Stark naked in the full moon light.
Your jasmine will remind me

Of your watermelon kisses that sweetened my lips,
And quenched my thirst long into the night...
And the stars up above when we made love
In the desert, in the heat,
On that full moon night.

     *Phil Pochurek*

# Humming in The Dark

She sat in her wrinkles and her wrinkled underwear,
On the edge of her bed in the midnight air,
Humming in the dark in the hint of a breeze.
Singing under a full moon, under the trees, familiar refrains.
The moonlight poured over her like quicksilver, like rain.
Covering all her bruises, hiding the stains of the day.
Patiently she sat in her underwear
Waiting for Jesus to take her away, take her where
The angels live and nobody feels any pain.
Her skin now hangs like gossamer veils
That barely cover the miles of trails of purple veins
That reads like a road map from a life long trip—
A story told from her head to the tip of her toes
Of a wonderful life slowly slipping away
And fading into white, humming at the moon
Long into the night waiting for the Lord to bring her home.
Never again would she be cold or alone,
Humming in the dark by the light of the moon...
Jesus would be coming soon to take our mother home.

# The Care Taker

His days are long,
His stooped form drawn.
At times I've heard him mumble
"I'm blessed with work
The whole day through as long
As I don't stumble or fall."
His routines, ingrained, simple.
Across seasons of care
Everywhere you look there
Is a touch of him.
He works in service in return
For graces known only to God.
His rewards are few
But his gifts are plenty.
He's blessed to be able to do
Everything thing that's asked of him,
And before each day is through
He gives thanks for one more day
For everything that comes his way.
In return, he takes care
To nourish and restore everything in his care,
Which he does diligently, respectfully, and more.
Working peacefully in the solitude of being alone,
His joy can be seen in his work, everywhere.
He tends the grounds year in, year out
As if they were his own.
He wouldn't have it any other way.
His work gives purpose to his life

And to him peace at the end of his day.
He learned a long time ago
That love is where your heart is
And his heart was in his work.
He learned that from his Maker,
The Builder of this fine earth...
And thanked Him often for all his blessings,
And finding his graces in being a caretaker
And the true value of his worth.

 *Phil Pochurek*

# I'm Always with You

I'll be the mirror you hold in your hand
Just to look in your eyes,
Just to gaze upon your face-
While you make all the right adjustments
To your makeup, to your lips, to your eyes,
Putting every hair in place.
I'll be the perfume you wear each day,
Just a drop between your beasts,
That makes you feel that special way
Whenever we caress.
A scent to remind you
Right next to your heart,
When I'm away from you
That we're never apart.
I'll be the silk you wear each night.
Can you feel your skin against mine?
With every step you take, every move you make,
I'll hold you close until the next time,
We are one.

# A Warriors Dance

A loon cried out as
They came to the lake
From out of the woods
Across green lawns,
Past picnic tables and swings
To the water's edge.
Not too silent but unseen, they dove in.
Of course, they were drunk
And naked as the full moon
That glistened on their chiseled bodies
While they swam laughing
All the way back to shore.
Like two ancient warriors with bodies cleansed
Their spirits were reborn.
Their hearts were open bared to each other
Unfettered by the lives that they led
Momentarily left behind them, in the dark.
They wrestled and howled long into the night.
Reuniting and bonding in spirit, in flesh.
Rolling on the grass, contemplating the moon,
Revisiting a past long before
The stars had their names.
Then dancing! Arms raised for flight,
They plunged back into the lake
Smooth as glass still warm from the sun.
Long into the night they swam as one
Under an ancient moon.
Their warriors dance over

Same as it had begun,
With the cry of a passing loon.



Phil Pochurek

# The Other Side
# of the River

# No Service Planned

She lived her life quietly, in the shadows.
He lived his life alone.
She preferred the late-night hours.
He was never home.
Her friend was always busy.
His friend never phoned.
She loved her cat and missed her mother.
He loved his dog and wished he knew his mother.
She volunteered at the mission on Sundays.
He spent his days off reading at a nursing home.
They never met.
Her family was gone.
He grew up in foster homes.
She died in her bed, in her sleep, alone.
He died at the ocean, on the sand.
They lived their lives out quietly
In the shadows of life.
They died alone together
There was no service planned.

# My Old Hands

Looking down I'm often reminded of
How old I must really be.
By my old hands at the end of my sleeves.
All gnarled and curled up like the exposed roots
Of an old Cyprus tree.
When I look down, I see my father's hands
And soon my grandfather's too.
Twisted and wrinkled from a lifetime of work
Doing what hands were meant to do.
From holding on and letting go
To tearing down and lifting up... too.
Always doing their best from what they know.
My old hands have stood the test of time
And are always ready to go, to reach out.
Still whole, complete, and hanging on
I'm blessed my old hands are still working fine.
They're hands that can still turn a page in the Bible
Or reach down and pick up a sidewalk dime,
But hands that can go stiff and ache with pain
Can still throw and catch a ball from time to time.
Still ache from all the work and tools
They've held onto throughout the years,
But can still pick up and hold a newborn baby
To wipe away their beading tears.
My old hands have been good to me
Like two old friends that were meant to be.
When I needed them were right in front of me
In a pocket or just hanging around.

Secure in their grip from their palms to their fingertips
Never once have my old hands let me down.
When I look down I'm often reminded
Over and over again
Of all the things I've let go of, held on to
And all the places my old hands have been,
And that every scar has a story.
From when my old hands were young and strong
Fearless in all their glory.

And now what will my old hands hold onto
That really matters most to me in the end.
For the rest of my everyday life?
A cup of coffee? The Bible? or maybe just a pen.
I already know what the most important
Thing of all will be.
It's the gentle touch from my loving wife
When she comes to take hold
Of my old hands from me.

       *Phil Pochurek*

# Run to Me

Run to me...
You wild creatures
In all your reckless abandon.
Like birds in flight
Your loving hearts bursting open
Your eyes flashing wide and bright.
Pouring all your intentions in my direction
Your feet barely hitting the ground.

Run to me...
Oh, heart of my hearts.
I've loved you both
Right from the start.
The moment I saw you,
You became a part of me.

Bring me all of your love
As fast as you can run
Unbridled, unshod and free,
And I'll be the one
With arms wide open
For you to run to me.

No greater joy
In all of Gods creatures
Have I found in Mother Nature
With all your loving doggone features
Has touched my soul

Like you...
Run to me
Run to me
Run to me

With your wild eyes and racing hearts,
And I'll be there to welcome you
With open arms into mine.
It's something I love to watch you do—
When you run to me,
Time after time, after time.



Phil Pochurek

# In the Company of Dogs

There's something to be said
  For the awareness that comes
From somebody who lives
Their whole lives at your knees
And eventually around your heart.
A perpetual toddler reaching up
Who's always trying to please.
A whole life that passes us by
In all its stages at our feet.
At your command to obey,
To meet your every wish.
Who willfully obliges me with a little play
For a belly rub and a full dish.
Whose time we share, though short to us,
Fills our lives beyond compare—
Endlessly with their love and trust.
When I look down my dogs are there
To say goodbye to say hello.
For all the times I come and go,
Their love is always the same.
As life goes on through all my years
I'm thankful I've been able to share
So many of them in the company of dogs.
Whenever I was short on love
They were always there.
From all their beginnings to every end
There isn't one I wouldn't go back to,
To do over again.

I've loved them all the same.
It's the company of dogs
That has filled in the holes in my life—
Moving me through to the end of my day
Helping me along the way to see.
Reminding me when I look down
There's always someone
Smiling around my knees.
That loves just being around and wants to please.
Who loves me every day.
Down by the river, out near or far,
In the company of dogs is where I'll be.

# I AM the Word

I always knew
That you were with me
But when I knocked
You were never home.
But now I know
You were always in me,
And since I've found you
I'm never alone.
I AM is God that burns within me,
Will always be and has always been.
When we pursue this holy fire
We'll never be alone again.
I AM the one who makes you happy.
I AM the one who brings you peace.
I AM the one who lives inside you, in love
Long before and ever after,
The first and last of your heartbeats.
I AM the servant and the master.
I AM the apple and the tree.
I AM God in everything,
On earth, in sky, on land and sea.
Look no further for my temple lies within you.
I AM the beat in every heart.
I've always been here for you to ask me
All your questions right from the start.
I AM the answer you've been seeking—
Unlock your heart and you will see.
I AM the fire that burns within you.

I AM you and you are me.
I AM God for ever and ever.
I AM the answer to the mystery.
I AM God and the glory—
Unlock your heart and set me free.
I AM grace, love, and forgiveness.
I AM the Word
And the Word is Me.

                Phil Pochurek

# The Only Words That Matter
# Are in Red

His voice had an earthly tone
You could believe in.
When He spoke to them with a calm determination.
His words were full of compassion
And with love.
For those who heard Him knew
It came from God above.

His words came down
Like a father to his children.
Whether spoken or
Written down in gilded pages.
To all of us who have heard them
They've remained the same,
As we bow our heads across the ages
And give thanks to the Lord
That He came.

Many books have been written
Of His journeys.
Many stories have been told
Of what He said.
Scribes and scholars have rebuked Him
For His teachings,
But the only words that matter are in Red.

Not all who knew Him
Feared His might and praised His glory
And saw His light shine
When He rose from out the grave.
But His promise was fulfilled for true believers—
Ask for forgiveness and like Him you will be saved.

Many books were written
Of the Messiahs coming,
And many more were written
After He was here
About the One who had risen from the dead.
And the value of those words
Will last forever but,
The only words that matter are in Red.

   *Phil Pochurek*

# Two Words

Walking along with my head bowed low
In full meditation,
Looking down as I go
Unaware of my direction,
The dogs know the way.
I wonder now the longer I live
Which one is harder?
To be obedient or to forgive.
On my journey down the road
To the truth.
Obedience and forgiveness.
Two words I never considered
In my youth
Now I think about them everyday.
The longer I live the more I know
But the harder it gets
For me to let go
Of my heart, my mind
When it's all I have left to show
For the life I've lived,
And I need them to find my way home.
Obedience keeps me from losing my mind
And forgiveness heals and helps me find
My heart along the way.
Without them I would be lost.
Had I only known them in my youth
I wouldn't have paid such a high price
And suffered what it cost me
To know the truth.

# Vegetarian Rumors

I heard the whispers late last night
Through the screen on my bedroom window.
It was still 85 degrees at midnight
And my freshly planted garden was on the grow.
My tomatoes share a bed with the cucumbers
That said they "were in the know."
My Early Girls said, "they were my favorites."
But the cucumbers said, "that wasn't so."
The girls said 'it really didn't matter
Just don't tell the squash or they won't grow."
Gossipy little plants those tomatoes
Whispering in the dark down below.
They said they "heard the eggplants had cross-pollinated
With the peppers but they'd have to wait until they show to see,
If they should have the Kohlrabi marry them."
They said they "heard it from the bees and they would know!"
Listening to my garden growing in the sultry moonlight heat
Kept my mind from drifting off
And made it hard to go back to sleep,
When there's so many vegetarian rumors to be heard
And so many secrets to keep.
In the raised bed gardens outside my window
Where the tomatoes and cucumbers share a bed
Whispering in the moonlight their vegetarian rumors
In the dark, in the dirt, "that's what they said."

# Jesus Had Four Legs

He leadeth me to walk down
By green pastures, past the cows
And along the river's edge.
To see if the quail and pheasants
Might be there
Hiding somewhere in the hedge.

He took me down into the river
To baptize Him
By throwing a stick
Over and over again.
So He could bring it back to me
Affirming His devotion and obedience.
And I could see
That His love for me
Would be there until the end.

There's no doubt in my mind
That Jesus was God.
And God spelled backwards
Is always dog.
My dog's name was Jesus
And He served me well
He certainly saved me
From a life in hell.
Each day was a lesson
I could never forget.
Our ministry began

As soon as we met.

From that first day
We walked together
He loved me faithfully without words.
Without hesitation He never strayed
And gave me His love and loved chasing birds,
His love was something I never betrayed.

He gave me His attention
Most of the time...
But always His obedience
Whenever He heard my voice.
He learned many words
But spoke none.
I know He would have if He had a choice.

He taught me about patience
Friendship, and loyalty
All without words,
And shared His joy with me
For His love of birds.

He served me an endless supply of dopamine
On our long walks

                    *Phil Pochurek*

From His ocean of unconditional love,
That washed over me daily.
So, I didn't have to take Xanax
To make it through my darkest days.

Jesus loved me
This I know
For His tail told me so.
And I loved Him back
As best I could
And followed Him where He would go.

Until the end on that fateful day
I had to leave without my friend
When God took Jesus far away
And Jesus became God again.

I know one day
My time will come
To join the Lord in His kingdom
To be with Jesus forever more
And to answer for all the things I've done.

I hope when Jesus comes for me
He brings a stick for me to throw

And all will be like it used to be.
Only this time no one will have to go
And we'll play together
For eternity.



Phil Pochurek

# Autumn Haze

Caught in the rising glance of a burgundy moon
Is the lenient odor of burning wheat.
Calico leaves play merrily in the forest,
Each their own painting,
Making a canvas of whatever they touch.
The moon, having long sense died,
Sheds his deathly pail light
Over an open meadow.
It here the deer have come to graze
In a breath of smoke,
In a rustle of leaves.
A most pleasing subtle autumn haze.

# Everyone Has a Story

# Everyone Has A Story

In the beginning we head down the road
Our windshields clean and clear.
Off on the road trip of our lives
To find out why we're here.
In our youth our pedal is to the metal
Fearlessly we drive into the night.
Hoping to find what we're looking for
Trying to do what's right.
Stopping we only deceive ourselves
Then check our mirrors for a little hindsight.
Give someone a helping hand
Here and there,
See if our tires need any air
And satisfy a few of our desires...
Help someone get a foot up in life
Maybe put out a few fires.
But the road is long no end in sight
As we begin to rack up the miles.
Everyone has a story to tell
Hidden behind their smiles.
Some are full of drama and tragedy,
Others of faith and glory.
Just under the surface
Or buried deep inside
Everyone has a story.
No matter how hard you try to escape
Don't let them hold you back.
For some too much is never enough,

For others life's an empty sack.
Whatever story your life becomes,
Wherever your road may take you
Our stories aren't for everyone,
But there's one who won't forsake you.
Every story ever told
All goes down in the same book.
All subject to the same review.
Written first on every heart
In the deepest part of you.
It's up to you to find your way... or not
And let your story do the telling,
In the end it's all you've got.
Your chapter in the Book of Life
Doesn't depend on how long you live
Or whether you won or lost,
But what you had to give.

     *Phil Pochurek*

# Too Late for Forgiveness

⸺ ❦ ⸺

Hurt feelings cloaked in anger
Tear and rent into a broken heart.
Too many years in the breaking.
Words spoken out of pain in haste.
Too late to take back what's been torn apart.
Too many years in the making.
Forsaking any reconciliation.
Words like cord wood thrown
Onto a fire, stoking the flames of pride.
Creating a divide
Too often, too large, too late
To reach across to the other side
And ask for forgiveness.
A fire so hot
It burned across the years.
So deep that time itself
Couldn't heal the wounds.
Embers smoldering so deep in a hurt
They never went out...
Or came to ash.

Until now.
Too bad the wood ran out
Before my pride did.
Now there's no one left on the other side
To beg for forgiveness.
To tell I'm sorry.
To reach across and make things right

Before they were gone forever.
Buried under a pile of ashes
Where a fire burned bright,
Lays a jagged scar
Across a broken heart full of regret.
Where the flames of pride burned tall.
Defeated in victory
By the prize itself...
Then cheated by death
I lost it all.



Phil Pochurek

# A Blessing for All Time

As I look around at this gathering tonight
I realize that something BIG is about to happen!
And today is just the beginning.
Something as perfect and natural
As the sunrise in the morning
Or the tide going out at the end of the day.
Dianna and John just seem to fit together
In that same natural and beautiful way.
I can only speak of what I know
From all the things I've seen
As I've watched this young lady
Blossom and grow into this beautiful bride—
The one you see before you today,
And all the years I've known her in between
To know that God has a plan.
And we have all come here to bear witness to
The bearing of His fruit.
The joining together of Dianna in His name
With this fine young man, John,
On this long-awaited day...
Who with his heart and soul has pledged
"Till death do us part in sickness and in health
For richer or poorer" all the obvious things
Of this earth and our daily lives
One can possibly give to another person
To profess their undying love,
Before God and all who are present.
Much more than anything else

This earth has to offer
Is this truth... that John loves Dianna
And Dianna loves John.
I'm sure as much as their mothers and fathers do.
Love each enough to become flesh of their flesh
To become one in their life
As they make it, build it
Going forward in the precious time
They have together, as one heart
On their journey down the road that lies ahead.
This is their love story for the ages.
To add to the book of life.
One that all who have gathered here today
Have a chapter in and now it's their turn
To add their pages into the book
We all know too well.
To write their story together
From this day forward as one
And ever after whatever may come,
The rest only time will tell.
Two young lives close to all of our hearts,
Some who have known them
Right from the start.

     *Phil Pochurek*

Mothers and fathers, sisters and brothers,
Friends and family all gathered here today
To bear witness to this union and pray
That their years together be plenty and long.
That whatever comes their way
They be strong and true to their promise
Made on this day to love each other
And stay true to their hearts.
Let God be their judge
And show them the way,
And rain down His blessings upon them
Forever and today.

# Looking Down

He never saw it coming.
He never heard a sound.
He never heard the shouts and screams
"Look out!" "Look up!" "Turn around!"
He had his earbuds in.
He was looking down.
He never played ball.
Rode a bike or learned to swim.
"You could get hurt!" "You could drown!"
Life in the real world scared him.
So, he started looking down.
Games and Podcasts filled his eyes and ears.
Then Instagram and selfies
Used any time that was left.
His hands never touched a book.
They said he was advanced for his years.
He could multitask with the best of them
He was a genius to his peers.
But never really got anything done.
His life was one big Instagram,
So he was always on the run.
And for all that time lost while he played
He paid the ultimate price
With the last step he would ever take.
And with that step he scored an extra life!
It would be his last mistake.
Too bad he couldn't use it now
To save him in real life!

He'd never been on an airplane
But in one step he was about to fly.
The car that hit him shot him thirty feet in the air,
Sent him a hundred feet down the road
And gave him his last look up at the sky.
The bone crushing impact was instantaneous.
He never really felt any pain.
One moment he was locked in mortal combat with Zanos,
The next he would never breathe again.
Everyone stopped for a moment
While they came to take him away.
The few that stopped took pictures,
But had nothing to say
As he lay there on the ground.
The rest that passed by didn't notice...
They were busy looking down.

     *Phil Pochurek*

# My Four-Legged Heart

My four-legged heart
Looks up at me with brown eyes
And pours herself into my soul
While we share my morning coffee.
Her years are beginning
To show on her face and in her step.
We both know
Her journey is almost over.
All her love now
Is in her eyes.
No more running and chasing.
No more long walks
Beside river canals and mountain streams.
No more running on the beach.
She runs in her dreams now.
And waits for me
Patiently with loving eyes
To do what must be done.
My four-legged heart knows
When it's time to go.
And the hardest part
Of loving a dog
Is always the goodbye...
Always.

# A Road to Nowhere

When pride becomes anger
And violence strikes out in fear
In an instant all ground that was gained is lost.
You can taste the electricity in the air
When sparks go flying
And words become visceral,
Cutting and slashing anyone who is near
That engages with them so all dialogue is lost.
Faces and names get lost in the rage,
It's the cost we pay when we're there.
There's nothing more to understand,
Nothing you can say that's right,
No mater how much you care.
No sense can be made when
Every word is a struggle and ends in a fight.
When all memory is lost with no end in sight
And that's only the beginning of the end
When the lucid distraction of common ground
Always seems to be just around the bend.
But every time you reach that turn
Something goes south, goes sideways again
And they're blinded with anger as they begin to slip
Back to where reality is just a memory
For those caught in dementia's grip.
Don't engage or you'll just enrage
Unless it's a risk you want to take.
Be loving, kind, and strong in your care
But don't make that mistake.

Remember they've forgotten more than you may know
And going home is all they want to do
Even when there's nowhere left to go,
And the person who looks like someone you once knew
Isn't even there.
Heading down a road to nowhere
Until all that's left is despair.

When the days of fighting are over
And there's no screaming and shouting anymore,
Just eating and sleeping all day long
With no memory from the moment before,
Something is terribly wrong.
How could something like this happen
To the ones we hold so dear?
Lost in their dementia until they're gone
Never satisfied with just being here.
Always trying to go home again...
Gotta go, gotta go, take me home!
To a home they'll never see.
Heading down a road to nowhere,
Hanging on to a memory,
Of a home that isn't there anymore
And never will be...

     *Phil Pochurek*

# At Last, An Orphan

What's left of
My sister is all over
My house now... literally.
And she's nowhere at all.
Just some of the things
She left behind at the end.
The gene we shared that
Made us gather, collect
Buy and store things,
Hoard the things we liked
From ceiling to floor
Is evident now, even more so
Everywhere in this room.
In the dishes we ate on, and
The Thanksgiving she blew up
When she let all of us know
How fucked up we were
Before she left.
Then came back at Christmas
And finished us off.
My sister could take
Mr. Rogers Neighborhood
And turn it into "August: Osage County"
at the turn of a phrase.
But now all that's left
Are some of the hard things she loved.
I saved a few of her
sweetest possessions.

A silver brush, an antique mirror...
Our mother's watch.
The few things she owned for years,
Touched and used over her lifetime.
They soften her spirit now, in my hands
And sweeten her memory through my tears,
Only my stubbornness was harder
Then her anger was hot
And it cost me a chance to ask
For her forgiveness at the end...forever.
And my last farewell.
Now I'll never know
How broken her heart really was
And she will never tell.
Her ashes are all I've got.



*Phil Pochurek*

# Ashes to Ashes Dust To Dust

We all began in much the same way.
In a drop of rain, in a flake of snow
Molded and shaped from a hand full of clay.
There's a rhythm, a sound inside us
In everything we do.
Breathe in breathe out, breathe in breathe out,
From God to us from me to you
Is pretty much what life is all about.
I've seen the light up in the sky
And the fire on the ground.
We live our lives somewhere in between...
Somewhere there's a meaning to be found.
In our youth the wind is in our face.
We're always running somewhere.
Never knowing, never caring what lies ahead.
At times it seems like we're running in place.
We're indestructible, immortal, and impatient.
Our virtues only beginning to line up
Until that moment, a tipping point in time,
When the wind shifts and moves behind us
Full on our backs
And we can feel our mortality
Breathing down our necks.
So, we dig our heals in
As it blows us from out of our comfort zones
In the warm familiarity of the present.
The land of the living
Towards our inevitable fate.

Down an unknown path that lies ahead.
A grandchild is born.
A parent or sibling passes
And someone you know has cancer...
With eyes wide open
We lean back into the winds of fate
And choose our steps with care.
Every heartbeat reminds us they have a number
And every breath is precious.
We eat more slowly,
We choose our words with care,
And listen more carefully to the world around us
And how lucky we are to be here.
Love is all that matters.
We race as humans
All towards the same end.
Our faith in God we trust...
All back to the beginning
To do it all again.
Ashes to ashes and dust to dust.

     *Phil Pochurek*

# A New Golden Calf

A light mist fell through the veil of a cloud
As it settled over the gathering below.
It was a familiar shroud... in Moses' day
Shuttering out the blue sky overhead.
Silencing its natural beauty in a Godly way
To see if anyone would look up instead.
We used to raise our arms
To the heavens and ask why
When we didn't know the answers for ourselves.
Raise our hands to pray.
Now we bow our heads
And pray with our thumbs
To a new Golden Calf,
That's in everyone's pocket today.
One we can hold in our hand.
No need for the sky
When we ask why to a digital god
As we bow our heads and say:
"Tell me what I want to know."
"What I should say?"
"How do I get to where I need to go."
"What should I believe in today?"
A silicone god that's always there
As long as you have a charge
With an answer for anything
You could ever ask
Its knowledge is omnisciently large.
Its speed is the new light

So certainly, it must be true.
If it's on the Internet where everything
Is right in front of you.
A digital god I can hold in my hand
Who's never let me down.
Who answers whenever I call.
Who's always there when I need them to be,
Yet not anywhere at all.
Off in a cloud I can hold in my hand
Where all good gods should be.
No wonder it's always raining
Down tears from the sky.
No one looks up for answers anymore
To ask their questions why.
We bow our heads
And pray with our thumbs
To get everything we need.
We get our answers by looking down.
No more soil of faith in the hearts of men
To grow our mustard seeds.
We count our wealth in gigabytes now,
It's the only memory we need.

It only took us a few hundred years
To surrender our souls to mankind.

     *Phil Pochurek*

How soon we've forgotten our Lord.
We pray with our thumbs now
To pocket prophets in the palms of our hands,
And no one ever gets bored.
Tapping out questions we use to ask Jesus
In an endless series of questions and demands...
Shamelessly we hide now in plain sight,
Pretending no one sees us.
Our god is conveniently stored in the cloud
Without worries where our souls are going
While the devil patiently waits to reap
The seeds that he's been sewing,
His Golden Calf is never wrong.
As we bow our heads with pride and pray with our thumbs
By proclaiming how right we are
In all the glory of our unknowing...
We bow our heads and pray with our thumbs
Not looking at where we're going.
With our new Golden Calf
In the palm of our hands
We pray to the Google, all knowing.

# With Heads Bowed Low

<hr>

With heads bowed low
No ones looking up anymore
With their hearts,
Their minds or their eyes.
It's no wonder no one knows
Where they're going.
Lost in their screens
Looking for answers and playing games.
It's no surprise everyone's
Become so all knowing.
We're constantly taking pictures
Of ourselves and our food.
In case we might forget
Who we are or what we ate
That we haven't noticed yet, we're getting lost.
Trying our best to get ahead or win
And not be late,
No one's noticed what it cost.

Somewhere down the pathway through mankind
With a handful of digital seeds
We planted the tree of technology,
Which helped us in the beginning
Save time and fulfill our needs.
But somewhere along the path
We lost out way
And the digital tree of knowledge grew.
Now everyone has a digital apple

In their hands from that tree
And we've all seemed to have forgotten
Everything we ever knew.
Instead of when asking questions
About something we want to know
Then looking up for ourselves to see
We're playing games, taking pictures of our food
Then turning our cameras on us
And shouting to the world
"Hey look at me."
We used to reach out to others
To give a helping hand.
Now we put our apples
On the end of a stick and shout
"Look at me I'm the greatest in the land."
And it all started with one byte.
The flavor of this knowledge
Soon created quite a demand.
To satisfy our desires
With the cries for more apples
And room for more bytes, we
Grew more desperate and louder
While the digital tree reached for the sky.
Bursting with knowledge in a flash of light
It gave birth to the digital cloud,

                    *Phil Pochurek*

Where everyone can shout and be
A star in their own digital sky:
"There is no God but look at me.
I'm here now and this is what I do!
Don't you all wish that you could be like me
Right now, instead of you?"
Everyone holds an apple now
That fell from that digital tree.
It's part of who we all are.
So,no one asks how anymore
How we could come so far
With our heads bowed low
Without looking up to see where we are,
Or where we should go.
With heads bowed low we pray to a god
Who lives in a digital cloud.
Asking questions from our most recent desires.
Hoping for answers to quench our thirst
For our latest cravings...
Only to create more fires.
By now we should have learned.
When you pray with your thumbs
Instead of your heart
You could end up getting burned
From a god who doesn't exist.

Stubborn in our pursuit of glory
We take another selfie and persist.
Without shame we eat from this tree
And its apple we hold in our hand.
Eating kilobytes and gigabytes as
We bow our heads across the land.
Asking questions from a god who doesn't exist.
Storing our answers in a digital cloud.
Next to all the pictures we've taken of ourselves
And all the dinners that we've had.
Looking for happiness in the palm of our hands
That can't be found,
Instead of looking up to the Lord.
Amen... how truly sad.
And yet we still persist...
With heads bowed low and an apple in our hand
We pray with our thumbs on a digital screen
All across the land to a god who doesn't exist.
With heads bowed low
And an apple in our hands...
We still persist.

 *Phil Pochurek*

# Sweet Bones

She's six pounds
Of fur covered carcass
When she's sleeping
Or on the prowl
With a voice like broken glass
Across a chalk board.
You can tell where she is
When she's up and about
From her earsplitting screeching howl.
For twenty one years she's been killing
Everything that crosses her path
That walks, crawls, or flies,
But she's too old now
To go out hunting and chasing anymore.
If she's not sleeping or eating,
She's taking a bath!

She's a well-traveled girl
Having lived in all our houses.
Minded three dogs and tolerated two other cats.
Chased, killed and eaten many "mouses"
And she's still alive...
She's out lived them all.
She still goes out climbing and exploring
On occasion, but she always
Comes back when I call.
Her screech is louder than she weighs.

Her spirit is warm
Held against my heart.
It's the only thing she owns
That isn't broken or torn apart,
And I wouldn't trade it for time or gold.
She's the softest thing
I've ever loved
That's loved me back
With four paws
That I've ever known.
And when she's finally gone
I'll miss those mournful cries
And those warm caresses
From her sweet bones.



*Phil Pochurek*

# The Edge of Tears

The older we get
The easier our walls come down.
Through the passing of years
It's often a blessing in disguise.
Which comes first as our memory goes:
Losing our vision or the telling of more lies.
The secrets we keep and the promises we've made
Over time take their toll on your heart.
Helping or hurting the ones you love
Trying to keep them from falling apart.
There's a picture of mom
Staring back at me from inside the bookcase
Right above Voltaire.
It was a hot summer day
Outside of her house and I remember being there.
She had her favorite purple dress on,
The one that she said she could wear
Because she was finally old enough to
And she really didn't care about
What any one thought of you.
She tried to smile in the midday sun
But it was too bright in her eyes.
She was on her way to church that day
But no matter how hard she'd try
She couldn't seem to go.
But she loved her dress,
Got dressed up any way
And hoped it didn't show.

She didn't know why for the last few years
That she seemed so fearful and confused,
And lately she always seemed to be
On the edge of tears.
Her health had been failing lately,
Over the years it had taken its toll,
And it was getting harder to get her breath.
It scared her more than it used to
And she became more preoccupied with death.
She talked on often about the good Lord
And about her younger years,
Saying some day soon He would come for her
And take away all her fears.
To join Him in the afterlife
After the living years.
She loved to talk about Jesus,
The Lord and all that he'd done,
And I would sit and listen to her every word
As long as she would go on
Knowing soon she would be gone.
I think of her often and miss her now
With just pictures to take her place,
And smile at all her memories
That time will never erase.
From the picture of her
Smiling down on me from the bookcase
In the passing of all the years...
On that Sunday afternoon in her purple dress,
Smiling on the edge of tears.

     *Phil Pochurek*

# Running on The Other side

Your days are spent now mostly sleeping
Off in dreams where old dogs go.
Running, chasing, on familiar paths
To the lakes and rivers, the ones you know.
Half blind, it's hard to see.
Half deaf, you don't always hear.
Some days you're doing better
And others you're too tired to care.
But in your dreams you're young again
Chasing seagulls on the beach,
Where from your bed comes muffled barks.
Legs flailing, eyes a flutter
Chasing something just out of reach.
It's an easy place for you to go to,
No aching muscles there.
You can run and bark all day long
And no one seems to care.
Then the laughter crashes in on you,
You've been chasing in your sleep.
Your dignity gone
But your soul lingers on,
While I pet you and quietly weep.
Now every time you close your eyes
You're where you want to be,
You sleep more now than you're awake
More than you're with me.
I'll miss you when you don't come back
From your favorite place to go to hide,

But I'll always know that you're waiting for me...
Running on the other side.



Phil Pochurek

www.ingramcontent.com/pod-product-compliance
Lightning Source LLC
Chambersburg PA
CBHW031259160726
47993CB00001B/226